OMAN'S QUIET DIPLOMACY: A BEACON OF PEACE AND STABILITY IN THE MIDDLE EAST

CONTENTS

Reconstruction support in conflict-affected countries:

Education and cultural exchange initiatives

Fostering cross-cultural understanding:

Promoting peace among younger generations:

Comparing Oman's quiet diplomacy to interventionist approaches

Assessing successes and limitations:

Drawing lessons from Oman's experience:

The future of Oman's peacemaking role

Evolving geopolitical dynamics:

Changing priorities of key international players:

INTRODUCTION

In recent years, I have developed a growing interest in understanding the intricate dynamics of the Middle East, a region often characterized by turmoil and conflict. Through my personal research, I have been particularly fascinated by the unique and inspiring story of the Sultanate of Oman, a small yet influential country that has played a significant role in spreading peace throughout the region. While larger and more powerful nations often dominate headlines, I believe it is essential to shed light on Oman's quiet diplomacy and constructive engagement, which have made it a beacon of stability in an otherwise volatile neighborhood.

In the following pages, I will share the findings of my personal exploration into Oman's history, foreign policy, and regional contributions, in an attempt to better understand how this nation has managed to maintain a peaceful presence and even foster reconciliation among its neighbors. By delving into the factors that have shaped Oman's diplomatic approach, as well as the challenges and opportunities it faces in the ever-changing landscape of the Middle East, I hope to provide a fresh perspective on the importance of promoting peace and understanding in a world that is all too often divided by conflict and misunderstanding.

As we embark on this journey to uncover the secrets of Oman's peaceful diplomacy, it is vital to begin by examining the foundations upon which the country's foreign policy has been built. The late Sultan Qaboos bin Said Al Said, who ruled Oman for nearly half a century, was the driving force behind the nation's peaceful and neutral stance. His visionary leadership and commitment to fostering understanding and cooperation among nations left a lasting legacy that continues to guide Oman's approach to regional and global affairs under the reign of his successor, Sultan Haitham bin Tariq Al Said.

Oman's strategic location, straddling the Gulf of Oman and the Arabian Sea, has made it a crucial player in regional trade and security. Its long coastline and proximity to vital shipping lanes have not only enabled Oman to cultivate strong economic ties with its neighbors but have also positioned the country as a key mediator in regional disputes. By maintaining a policy of neutrality and non-interference, Oman has been able to establish trust with conflicting parties, paving the way for constructive dialogue and conflict resolution.

The nation's commitment to cultural diplomacy and interfaith dialogue has also played a crucial role in promoting peace and understanding in the Middle East. Through initiatives that foster cross-cultural exchange and respect for diversity, Oman has been able to build bridges between different religious and ethnic groups, helping to reduce tensions and promote social cohesion within the region.

Despite its successes, Oman faces several challenges in maintaining its role as a peacemaker in the Middle East. Balancing relations with regional and global powers, addressing domestic issues, and navigating an increasingly complex geopolitical landscape are just a few of the hurdles that the Sultanate must overcome. Nevertheless, Oman's quiet diplomacy and steadfast commitment to peace offer valuable lessons for other nations seeking to contribute to stability and harmony in the world.

In the sections that follow, we will delve deeper into the various aspects of Oman's peaceful diplomacy and examine the factors that have contributed to its success, as well as the challenges and opportunities that lie ahead. By sharing this personal research, I hope to inspire further inquiry into Oman's unique approach to regional peace and the potential for its replication in other parts of the world, where conflict and misunderstanding continue to divide communities and nations.

NEUTRALITY AND NON-INTERFERENCE IN OMAN'S FOREIGN POLICY

The Significance of Neutrality and Non-Interference in Oman's Foreign Policy

Oman's foreign policy has long been characterized by a unique commitment to neutrality and non-interference, setting it apart from other countries in the tumultuous Middle East. This principled approach has played a crucial role in enabling the nation to maintain good relations with various regional actors, establish itself as a trusted mediator, and contribute to peace and stability in the region. The following paragraphs explore how Oman's avoidance of regional alliances, proxy wars, and confrontational policies has shaped its foreign policy and facilitated its vital role as a mediator and peacemaker in the Middle East.

AVOIDING REGIONAL ALLIANCES:

Oman's foreign policy is uniquely characterized by a steadfast commitment to neutrality and non-interference, as demonstrated by its consistent refusal to join multi-national political and military coalitions in the tumultuous Middle East. This principled approach has been instrumental in enabling the nation to maintain an independent and balanced stance in its foreign relations, fostering goodwill among various regional actors, and ensuring open lines of communication with diverse parties.

Throughout its modern history, Oman has successfully withstood pressure to join regional alliances or adopt a more confrontational posture towards its neighbors. By eschewing these aggressive strategies, Oman has instead pursued a pragmatic and inclusive foreign policy that places a premium on dialogue, cooperation, and mutual respect. This approach has not only bolstered Oman's reputation as a reliable and trustworthy partner on the international stage, but it has also been pivotal in facilitating its vital role as a mediator and peacemaker in the region.

Oman's decision to maintain a neutral stance in its foreign policy has allowed it to navigate the complexities of the Middle East with remarkable success. By abstaining from taking sides in the myriad conflicts and disputes that have embroiled the region, Oman has managed to avoid alienating potential allies or entrenching itself in intractable situations. This equidistant approach to regional politics has not only enabled Oman to engage with all parties involved in various conflicts but has also granted it a unique position from which to broker peace and understanding.

Moreover, Oman's commitment to neutrality and non-interference has engendered a sense of trust and respect among its neighbors, making the nation a sought-after partner in diplomatic efforts aimed at defusing regional tensions. Oman's pragmatic and inclusive foreign policy has been instrumental in creating an environment conducive to dialogue and negotiation, even in the face of seemingly intractable disagreements between regional actors.

In conclusion, Oman's foreign policy, characterized by its unwavering commitment to neutrality and non-interference, has played a crucial role in enabling the nation to maintain an independent and balanced stance in its foreign relations. By fostering goodwill and maintaining open lines of communication with diverse regional actors, Oman has been able to establish itself as a reliable and trustworthy partner, ultimately facilitating its vital role as a mediator and peacemaker in the Middle East.

STEERING CLEAR OF PROXY WARS:

Oman's strategic decision to abstain from participating in conflicts involving regional powers has been a crucial aspect of its policy of neutrality and non-interference. This commitment has enabled the country to maintain a neutral and impartial stance on various issues affecting the Middle East, effectively sidestepping the intricate web of rivalries, tensions, and power struggles that often characterize the region.

By consciously choosing not to engage in proxy wars, Oman has successfully avoided the pitfalls associated with militarized and confrontational foreign policies, which often result in increased regional instability and suffering. This decision has further allowed Oman to concentrate its efforts on promoting diplomacy, dialogue, and cooperation as the primary means of resolving disputes and conflicts in the Middle East.

Owing to its non-involvement in regional conflicts, Oman has frequently been regarded as a neutral arbiter and trusted mediator in situations where other countries may be perceived as having vested interests or biases. This unique positioning has enabled Oman to play a crucial role in facilitating communication between warring parties, hosting peace talks, and promoting mutual understanding among nations with differing political, religious, or ideological backgrounds.

Oman's policy of neutrality and non-interference, demonstrated by its avoidance of regional alliances and proxy wars, has served as the bedrock of the nation's foreign policy approach. This steadfast commitment has allowed the Sultanate to cultivate and maintain strong relations with a diverse array of regional actors, develop an image of impartiality and trustworthiness, and play a vital role in promoting peace and stability in the Middle East.

Moreover, Oman's neutral foreign policy has garnered international respect, allowing it to wield soft power and contribute to global peace initiatives. As an advocate for peaceful resolutions to conflicts, Oman has emerged as a leading voice in the region, urging other nations to adopt similar diplomatic approaches in their foreign policies. The success of Oman's approach serves as a model for other nations navigating the complexities of geopolitics, highlighting the potential benefits of maintaining neutrality and non-interference.

In conclusion, Oman's policy of neutrality and non-interference, exemplified by its avoidance of regional alliances and proxy wars, has been a cornerstone of the nation's foreign policy approach. By maintaining good relations with a diverse range of regional actors, cultivating an image of impartiality and trustworthiness, and focusing on diplomacy and dialogue, Oman has played a vital role in promoting peace and stability in the Middle East and beyond.

THE INFLUENCE OF OMANI LEADERSHIP ON DIPLOMACY

The Sultanate of Oman's diplomacy has been significantly shaped by its leaders, who have consistently emphasized the principles of neutrality and non-interference. This chapter delves into the impact of two key Omani leaders on the nation's diplomatic approach: the late Sultan Qaboos and his successor, Sultan Haitham bin Tariq.

SULTAN QABOOS'S IMPACT:

Sultan Qaboos bin Said al Said, who ascended to the throne in 1970, played a pivotal and transformative role in shaping Oman's policy of neutrality and non-interference. Through his visionary leadership, the nation not only emerged from isolation but also embarked on a path of modernization and development. Simultaneously, Sultan Qaboos fostered friendly relations with nations around the world, irrespective of their political or ideological differences, building a foundation of trust and credibility among regional and global actors.

Sultan Qaboos's visionary leadership was characterized by his unwavering commitment to diplomacy and dialogue in foreign policy. By prioritizing peaceful and diplomatic means of resolving conflicts and disputes, Oman was able to cultivate a reputation as a reliable and impartial partner in the international community. This approach allowed the nation to foster constructive relationships with other countries, even in a region often fraught with tension and strife.

Modernization and reform were also key aspects of Sultan Qaboos's reign. He initiated numerous efforts to modernize Oman's economy, infrastructure, and institutions, which significantly enhanced the nation's capacity to engage more effectively in international diplomacy. Under his leadership, Oman underwent a comprehensive transformation that touched upon every aspect of society, from education and healthcare to governance and economic diversification. These reforms not only improved the quality of life for the Omani people but also demonstrated the nation's commitment to progress and development.

Sultan Qaboos's tenure also saw Oman gain recognition for its role in mediation and conflict resolution. Under his guidance, the nation played an active and prominent role in addressing various regional and international conflicts, leveraging its impartiality and trustworthiness to facilitate dialogue between conflicting parties. Oman's diplomatic efforts, including its involvement in the Iran nuclear deal negotiations and attempts to mediate between Iran and Saudi Arabia, further solidified its status as a key player in promoting peace and stability in the region.

In conclusion, Sultan Qaboos bin Said al Said's transformative leadership had a lasting impact on Oman's policy of neutrality and non-interference. His commitment to diplomacy, dialogue, modernization, and reform enabled the nation to establish a strong foundation for international relations, enhance its capacity for diplomatic engagement, and gain recognition for its role in mediation and conflict resolution. Sultan Qaboos's legacy continues to influence Oman's approach to diplomacy, serving as an example of the potential benefits of peaceful and constructive engagement in a turbulent world.

SULTAN HAITHAM BIN TARIQ'S APPROACH:

Sultan Haitham bin Tariq al Said, who succeeded Sultan Qaboos in 2020, has continued to promote Oman's diplomatic principles, building upon his predecessor's legacy. As a result, Oman remains steadfast in its role as a peacemaker and mediator in the region, even as the geopolitical landscape continues to evolve and present new challenges.

Upholding the principles of neutrality and non-interference: Sultan Haitham has resolutely maintained Oman's long-standing policy of neutrality and non-interference, which has been instrumental in preserving the nation's stability and fostering constructive relationships with other countries. By adhering to these guiding principles, Oman has been able to navigate complex regional dynamics while maintaining its reputation as an impartial and trustworthy actor.

Strengthening regional partnerships: Recognizing the importance of collaboration in addressing regional challenges, Sultan Haitham has focused on deepening Oman's ties with its neighbors and other regional powers. This commitment to building strong partnerships has further enhanced the nation's credibility and influence in diplomatic affairs, enabling Oman to play a more prominent role in promoting regional cooperation and dialogue.

Addressing contemporary challenges: Under Sultan Haitham's leadership, Oman has continued to engage in diplomatic efforts aimed at addressing pressing regional and global issues. These efforts include working towards peaceful resolutions to ongoing conflicts in Yemen and Syria, as well as tackling broader concerns related to climate change, terrorism, and economic development. By actively participating in discussions and initiatives on these critical topics, Oman demonstrates its dedication to fostering a more stable and prosperous regional environment.

Promoting cultural diplomacy and interfaith dialogue: Sultan Haitham has also emphasized the importance of cultural diplomacy and interfaith dialogue as a means of promoting tolerance, understanding, and peace among diverse religious and ethnic groups in the region. By encouraging respectful and inclusive exchanges, Oman fosters an atmosphere of mutual respect and understanding, which serves as a foundation for lasting peace and cooperation.

In conclusion, the influence of Omani leadership on diplomacy has been profound and enduring. Both the late Sultan Qaboos and his successor, Sultan Haitham bin Tariq, have played pivotal roles in shaping Oman's policy of neutrality and non-interference, fostering friendly relations with all nations, and strengthening the nation's role as a peacemaker and mediator in the region. As a result, Oman stands as a shining example of the power of diplomacy and dialogue in promoting peace and stability in an often tumultuous part of the world, inspiring hope for a more harmonious future.

OMAN'S MEDIATION EFFORTS

Oman's diplomatic approach, characterized by neutrality and non-interference, has uniquely positioned the country to serve as a mediator in various regional conflicts and negotiations. The Sultanate has consistently leveraged its credibility and impartiality to bring conflicting parties to the table, fostering dialogue and promoting peaceful resolutions. This chapter will explore some of the most significant examples of Oman's mediation efforts, focusing on its role in the Iran nuclear deal and its attempts to facilitate dialogue between Iran and Saudi Arabia.

THE IRAN NUCLEAR DEAL:

During the formative stages of the Iran nuclear deal negotiations, Oman's discreet yet critical role in facilitating initial talks between Iran and the United States proved invaluable. These early discussions set the stage for the historic 2015 Joint Comprehensive Plan of Action (JCPOA), an agreement designed to address international concerns over Iran's nuclear program and curb the proliferation of nuclear weapons in the region.

1. Secret negotiations: The power of Oman's discreet diplomacy came to the fore when it brought Iran and the United States together for clandestine negotiations in 2012 and 2013. Oman's provision of a neutral venue for these discussions was crucial in building trust and fostering an atmosphere that was conducive to open dialogue.

2. Building confidence: Oman's subtle yet effective diplomatic approach facilitated the exchange of letters between the United States and Iran, helping to establish direct communication between the two nations and paving the way for further engagement.

3. Oman's unique position: As a result of the Sultanate's long-standing amicable relations with both Iran and the United States, Oman was able to act as an impartial intermediary, bridging the gap between the two countries and encouraging constructive dialogue on a highly sensitive and complex issue.

4. The role of Omani leadership: Oman's ability to serve as a diplomatic bridge can be attributed, in part, to the vision and leadership of the late Sultan Qaboos bin Said al Said, who was committed to promoting peace and stability in the region.

5. The impact of the JCPOA: The successful conclusion of the Iran nuclear deal, made possible in part by Oman's quiet diplomacy, marked a significant milestone in efforts to ensure nuclear non-proliferation and promote regional stability. The JCPOA not only placed constraints on Iran's nuclear program but also initiated a process of engagement between Iran and the international community, fostering a more cooperative regional environment.

6. Challenges and setbacks: Despite the success of the JCPOA, the agreement has faced numerous challenges and setbacks, including the United States' withdrawal from the deal in 2018 and ongoing tensions between Iran and its regional neighbors. Nevertheless, Oman's role in facilitating the initial negotiations stands as a testament to the effectiveness of its diplomatic approach in navigating complex geopolitical issues.

In summary, Oman's discreet diplomacy was instrumental in the early stages of the Iran nuclear deal negotiations, as it enabled Iran and the United States to engage in crucial discussions that ultimately led to the JCPOA. Oman's unique position and its commitment to neutrality and non-interference allowed it to act as an impartial intermediary, fostering dialogue on a highly sensitive issue and contributing to regional stability.

IRAN-SAUDI ARABIA DIALOGUE:

In recent years, as tensions between Iran and Saudi Arabia have escalated, Oman has taken on the role of a diplomatic facilitator, seeking to promote dialogue and cooperation between the two regional powers. The Sultanate has capitalized on its impartiality and credibility to arrange talks aimed at reducing tensions and addressing key issues of contention.

1. Hosting talks: Oman has hosted multiple rounds of talks between Iranian and Saudi officials, providing a neutral and discreet platform for dialogue between the two rivals. These talks have offered an opportunity for both sides to air grievances, explore areas of mutual interest, and seek common ground.

2. Building trust: Oman's diplomatic efforts have focused on fostering trust between Iran and Saudi Arabia, as it is an essential prerequisite for meaningful dialogue and cooperation. Oman's unique position as a friend to both nations has allowed it to serve as an honest broker in these delicate discussions.

3. Promoting regional stability: By fostering communication between Iran and Saudi Arabia, Oman seeks to defuse tensions that threaten regional stability and exacerbate existing conflicts. The Sultanate's mediation efforts are aimed at promoting a more

peaceful and cooperative regional environment, which would benefit not only the two rivals but also the broader Middle East.

4. Engaging regional and international stakeholders: Oman's diplomatic outreach has extended beyond Iran and Saudi Arabia, as it recognizes the importance of engaging other regional and international stakeholders in its efforts to promote dialogue and cooperation. By doing so, Oman seeks to create a broader consensus and encourage collective action in addressing regional challenges.

5. Challenges and setbacks: Despite Oman's mediation efforts, progress has been slow and fraught with challenges, as deep-seated mistrust and competing interests continue to hinder dialogue and cooperation between Iran and Saudi Arabia. Ongoing conflicts in Yemen and Syria, as well as proxy battles in various parts of the region, have further complicated the process of reconciliation.

6. The importance of perseverance: Despite these setbacks, Oman remains committed to its role as a mediator, recognizing that peace and stability in the region can only be achieved through sustained dialogue and compromise. The Sultanate's unwavering dedication to its diplomatic efforts highlights the importance of perseverance in the face of seemingly insurmountable challenges.

In conclusion, Oman's efforts to promote dialogue and cooperation between Iran and Saudi Arabia showcase the power of diplomacy and the significance of impartial mediation in addressing regional tensions. While progress has been slow, Oman's commitment to fostering communication and building trust between the two rivals offers hope for a more stable and peaceful future in the Middle East.

STRATEGIC SIGNIFICANCE OF OMAN'S LOCATION

Oman's unique geographical position, straddling the Gulf of Oman and the Arabian Sea, has significant implications for its foreign policy, its role in regional cooperation, and its capacity to prevent conflicts. As a key player in the Middle East, Oman leverages its strategic location to promote collaborative efforts, economic integration, and maritime security among its neighbors.

REGIONAL COOPERATION:

Trade and economic integration: Oman's prime location has been instrumental in fostering the development of robust trade links and economic integration with neighboring countries. Its strategic position along vital shipping routes, coupled with the establishment of modern ports and infrastructure projects, has significantly enhanced regional connectivity. This, in turn, has stimulated economic growth both within the Sultanate and throughout the broader Middle East. By encouraging cross-border collaboration, Oman plays a pivotal role in promoting economic cooperation and resilience in the region.

Energy security: Oman's close proximity to major oil and gas producers in the Persian Gulf, such as Saudi Arabia, Iran, and the United Arab Emirates, has enabled it to play a critical role in maintaining energy security in the region. By ensuring the safe passage of energy resources through its territorial waters, Oman not only safeguards regional energy supplies but also contributes to the stability of global energy markets. This, in turn, helps to maintain the overall economic well-being of countries that depend on these resources.

Diplomatic ties: Oman's strategic location has allowed it to cultivate and maintain close diplomatic ties with a diverse array of regional actors, including Iran, Saudi Arabia, and the United Arab Emirates. Its balanced approach to foreign policy, combined with its geographical advantages, has positioned the Sultanate as a trusted mediator and facilitator of dialogue in various regional disputes. Oman's ability to engage with different political, religious, and cultural factions in the Middle East demonstrates the country's commitment to peace and stability in the region. By fostering constructive dialogue and maintaining strong diplomatic relations, Oman plays a crucial role in promoting understanding and collaboration among its neighbors, ultimately contributing to a more stable and prosperous Middle East.

CONFLICT PREVENTION:

Maritime security: Oman's strategic location allows it to play a pivotal role in monitoring and preventing maritime disputes in the region. Its navy and coast guard work closely with regional partners to ensure the security of key shipping lanes, combat piracy, and address issues such as illegal fishing and smuggling. By maintaining a strong maritime presence, Oman helps to safeguard vital sea routes and contributes to the overall stability and security of the region.

Facilitating communication: Oman's position at the crossroads of the Arabian Sea and the Gulf of Oman allows it to serve as a communication hub between regional actors, both in times of peace and during crises. This unique advantage enhances Oman's ability to act as a mediator and helps to prevent misunderstandings and miscommunications that could escalate into conflicts. In addition, Oman's role as a facilitator of dialogue demonstrates its commitment to fostering cooperation and building bridges among countries in the region.

Military cooperation: Oman's strategic location has led to the development of strong military ties with regional and global powers, including the United States and the United Kingdom. These partnerships enable Oman to participate in joint military exercises, share intelligence, and collaborate on security initiatives, further enhancing its capacity to prevent and manage conflicts in the region. Such military cooperation also bolsters Oman's defense capabilities, ensuring that it is well-prepared to address any threats to its own territorial integrity or the broader regional stability.

Humanitarian assistance: Oman's location also places it in a prime position to provide humanitarian assistance during crises and natural disasters. The Sultanate has a history of extending aid to neighboring countries in times of need, whether in response to man-made conflicts or natural catastrophes. By offering humanitarian support, Oman not only helps to alleviate suffering but also contributes to regional stability by demonstrating solidarity and fostering goodwill among nations.

In conclusion, Oman's strategic location has significant implications for its role in regional cooperation, conflict prevention, and humanitarian assistance. By leveraging its geographical advantages and maintaining strong ties with regional and global partners, Oman plays a crucial role in promoting peace, stability, and prosperity in the Middle East.

CULTURAL DIPLOMACY AND INTERFAITH DIALOGUE

In a region often characterized by religious and cultural divisions, Oman stands out for its commitment to promoting tolerance, understanding, and respect for diversity. The Sultanate's emphasis on cultural diplomacy and interfaith dialogue has played a significant role in fostering a more harmonious and inclusive environment in the Middle East.

PROMOTING TOLERANCE:

The importance of culture in diplomacy: Oman recognizes that culture is a powerful tool in fostering mutual understanding, building bridges between nations, and promoting peaceful coexistence. By engaging in cultural diplomacy, the Sultanate seeks to project a positive image of its society, values, and traditions while highlighting its commitment to dialogue and cooperation.

Cultural initiatives and exchanges: Oman has invested in various cultural initiatives, both at home and abroad, to showcase its rich heritage and promote cross-cultural understanding. These efforts include hosting cultural events, supporting artistic and educational programs, and participating in international cultural festivals.

ENCOURAGING UNDERSTANDING:

Oman's commitment to religious tolerance: The Sultanate is a predominantly Muslim country, but it is also home to diverse religious and ethnic groups. Oman's commitment to religious tolerance is enshrined in its constitution, which guarantees freedom of worship for all residents.

Interfaith initiatives and institutions: The government has established and supported numerous institutions and initiatives aimed at fostering interfaith dialogue and promoting respect for religious diversity. These efforts include the Sultan Qaboos Grand Mosque, which serves as a hub for religious learning and dialogue, and the establishment of a dedicated Ministry of Religious Affairs to oversee matters related to religious tolerance and understanding.

NCOURAGING UNDERSTANDING THROUGH CULTURAL INSTITUTIONS AND INITIATIVES

The Sultan Qaboos Grand Mosque: This architectural marvel serves not only as a place of worship but also as a center for learning and interfaith dialogue. The mosque's library houses an extensive collection of religious texts, representing various faiths and fostering a spirit of inquiry and understanding among visitors.

The Royal Opera House Muscat: As a leading cultural institution in the region, the Royal Opera House Muscat showcases both local and international artistic talent, hosting performances that celebrate cultural diversity and foster mutual appreciation for the arts. By providing a platform for artistic expression, the Royal Opera House helps to break down cultural barriers and promote understanding among different communities.

Educational initiatives: Oman invests in various educational initiatives aimed at promoting cultural exchange and understanding among its citizens and the broader international community. This includes supporting scholarships and exchange programs for students, academics, and artists, as well as sponsoring cultural events and exhibitions that showcase the diversity of Omani society.

CHALLENGES FACED BY OMAN IN ITS PEACEMAKING ROLE.

As a mediator and peacemaker in the Middle East, Oman has earned a reputation for its commitment to neutrality, non-interference, and dialogue. However, the Sultanate faces several challenges in its efforts to maintain this role, including balancing relations with regional and global powers and addressing domestic issues that may impact its diplomatic capacity.

BALANCING RELATIONS WITH REGIONAL AND GLOBAL POWERS:

Navigating the complex geopolitical landscape: Oman's location in the heart of the Middle East means that it must navigate a complex geopolitical landscape, characterized by shifting alliances, rivalries, and tensions. The Sultanate's challenge lies in maintaining good relations with all countries while upholding its principles of neutrality and non-interference.

Managing relations with regional rivals: The Middle East is home to several competing powers, such as Iran and Saudi Arabia, whose rivalry often threatens regional stability. Oman must balance its relations with these nations carefully, ensuring that its diplomatic efforts do not provoke suspicion or hostility from either side.

Engaging with global powers: Oman also maintains relations with global powers like the United States, Russia, and China, each of which has its own interests and agendas in the region. The Sultanate must navigate these relationships skillfully, working to maintain its neutral stance and avoid becoming entangled in broader geopolitical struggles.

ADDRESSING DOMESTIC ISSUES:

Economic diversification: Oman's economy is heavily reliant on hydrocarbon resources, making it vulnerable to fluctuations in global energy markets. The government must work towards diversifying the economy to ensure long-term stability and sustainable growth, which in turn will help maintain the country's diplomatic capacity.

Social development: The Sultanate faces several social challenges, such as unemployment, particularly among its youth population, and the need to provide adequate housing, education, and healthcare for its citizens. Addressing these issues is essential to maintaining social harmony and stability, which are vital to Oman's continued success as a diplomatic actor in the region.

Political reforms: Oman has made strides in political reform, but further efforts are needed to ensure transparency, inclusiveness, and the rule of law. Strengthening democratic institutions and promoting good governance will not only bolster the nation's domestic stability but also enhance its credibility as a mediator and peacemaker on the international stage.

OMAN'S ROLE IN REGIONAL ECONOMIC INTEGRATION

Oman plays a significant role in promoting regional economic integration in the Middle East. Through its involvement in the Gulf Cooperation Council (GCC), support for regional infrastructure projects, and commitment to economic diplomacy, the Sultanate actively encourages collaboration, trade, investment, and interdependence among neighboring nations, thereby fostering peace and stability in the region.

GULF COOPERATION COUNCIL:

Promoting economic collaboration: As a member of the GCC, Oman works closely with other member countries to enhance economic collaboration, facilitate trade, and stimulate investment within the region. This cooperation is essential to fostering a strong and prosperous regional economy, which in turn can help to promote stability and security.

Establishing common economic policies: Oman plays an active role in shaping and implementing common economic policies within the GCC, such as the harmonization of trade regulations and the coordination of fiscal policies. These shared policies help to create an integrated economic environment, enabling the free flow of goods, services, and capital across the region.

Enhancing regional security: The GCC also serves as a platform for security cooperation among its member states. By working together on issues such as counterterrorism, defense, and cybersecurity, Oman and its GCC partners can strengthen regional security and create a more stable environment for economic growth.

INFRASTRUCTURE PROJECTS:

Transportation networks: Oman actively supports the development of regional transportation networks, including roads, railways, and ports. These projects not only enhance connectivity within the Middle East but also foster economic growth and interdependence among nations in the region.

Energy systems: Oman is involved in regional energy projects, such as the construction of cross-border electricity grids and the development of natural gas infrastructure. These initiatives help to ensure the reliable and efficient supply of energy resources throughout the region, which is critical to sustaining economic growth and stability.

ECONOMIC TIES FOR PEACE AND STABILITY:

Encouraging trade and investment: Oman promotes economic diplomacy by encouraging trade, investment, and economic cooperation between countries with divergent political and ideological orientations. By fostering economic interdependence, the Sultanate aims to create an environment conducive to peace, understanding, and stability in the Middle East.

Building trust and mutual understanding: Oman's commitment to economic diplomacy helps to build trust and mutual understanding among regional actors. As countries engage in trade and investment, they become more aware of their shared interests and the potential benefits of collaboration, which can contribute to the reduction of tensions and the resolution of conflicts.

Fostering regional resilience: Economic integration can help to build regional resilience by promoting economic diversification and reducing dependence on a single resource or market. This resilience, in turn, can contribute to greater stability and security in the region.

ADDRESSING TRANSNATIONAL CHALLENGES

In today's interconnected world, transnational challenges such as terrorism, piracy, and human trafficking require a coordinated and cooperative approach to effectively address them. Oman, as a responsible member of the international community, has taken various measures to tackle these issues by collaborating with regional and global partners, sharing intelligence, and participating in initiatives to counter these threats. This chapter will explore Oman's role in addressing transnational challenges and the strategies it employs to maintain regional stability and security.

COUNTERING TERRORISM:

Collaborative approach: Oman's approach to combating terrorism involves close collaboration with regional and international partners. The nation shares intelligence, coordinates security efforts, and participates in regional and international initiatives to counter violent extremism and dismantle terrorist networks.

Capacity building: Oman invests in capacity building programs to enhance the skills and expertise of its security forces, law enforcement agencies, and other relevant stakeholders. These efforts contribute to the nation's ability to effectively detect, prevent, and respond to terrorist threats.

Preventing radicalization: Oman works to address the root causes of terrorism by promoting social cohesion, religious tolerance, and economic development. By creating an inclusive society and providing opportunities for its citizens, the nation helps to mitigate the risk of radicalization and extremism.

COMBATING PIRACY:

Maritime security cooperation: Oman cooperates with regional and international partners to ensure maritime security and prevent piracy in the waters surrounding the Arabian Peninsula. This collaboration includes joint naval patrols, intelligence sharing, and coordinated efforts to protect vital sea routes that are critical to the global economy.

Capacity building and training: Oman invests in capacity building and training programs for its navy and coast guard, enhancing their ability to respond to maritime security threats, including piracy. This helps to ensure the safety and security of the nation's territorial waters and the broader maritime domain.

Legal framework: Oman has developed a robust legal framework to prosecute and punish pirates and those involved in piracy-related activities. By implementing strong anti-piracy laws, the nation demonstrates its commitment to addressing this transnational challenge and upholding the rule of law.

OMAN'S FOREIGN AID AND HUMANITARIAN ASSISTANCE

Oman has consistently demonstrated its commitment to peace and stability in the Middle East by providing foreign aid and humanitarian assistance to conflict-affected countries in the region. This chapter will explore Oman's peacebuilding efforts, support for reconstruction initiatives, and commitment to providing humanitarian assistance to vulnerable populations in war-torn nations.

PEACEBUILDING EFFORTS:

Financial and material support: Oman's provision of financial and material support to peacebuilding and reconstruction initiatives in conflict-affected countries, such as Yemen and Syria, reflects the nation's dedication to fostering stability in the region. This support includes funding for infrastructure projects, social services, and capacity building initiatives aimed at promoting sustainable development and lasting peace.

Diplomatic engagement: In addition to providing financial and material support, Oman actively engages in diplomatic efforts to facilitate dialogue and negotiation between conflicting parties. By leveraging its impartiality and credibility, the Sultanate plays an important role in mediating disputes and fostering dialogue that can lead to peaceful resolutions.

Capacity building: Oman invests in capacity building programs to strengthen the ability of conflict-affected countries to address their challenges and build sustainable peace. These programs focus on areas such as governance, security sector reform, and economic development, enabling countries to build the foundations for long-term stability.

RECONSTRUCTION SUPPORT IN CONFLICT-AFFECTED COUNTRIES:

Infrastructure development: Oman recognizes the importance of rebuilding infrastructure in conflict-affected countries as a critical component of post-conflict recovery. The Sultanate supports initiatives aimed at reconstructing vital facilities, such as schools, hospitals, and transportation networks, which contribute to improved living conditions and social stability.

Economic revitalization: Oman supports efforts to revitalize the economies of war-torn nations by promoting trade, investment, and economic cooperation. By encouraging economic growth and job creation, the Sultanate helps to foster an environment conducive to peace and prosperity.

Social development: Oman is committed to promoting social development in conflict-affected countries by supporting initiatives focused on education, healthcare, and community resilience. These efforts help to address the underlying causes of conflict and create the conditions necessary for sustainable peace.

EDUCATION AND CULTURAL EXCHANGE INITIATIVES

Education and cultural exchange initiatives play a vital role in bridging divides between different communities and promoting peace in the Middle East. Oman, recognizing the importance of these endeavors, actively promotes educational exchanges, partnerships, and youth-oriented programs that foster cross-cultural understanding and empower future generations to become agents of peace and positive change in the region.

FOSTERING CROSS-CULTURAL UNDERSTANDING:

Educational exchanges and partnerships: Oman actively supports educational exchanges and partnerships with institutions in the region and beyond. By facilitating the sharing of knowledge, ideas, and experiences, these exchanges help to deepen understanding and appreciation for the diverse cultures, traditions, and perspectives that exist within the Middle East and across the globe.

Scholarships and study abroad programs: The Sultanate offers scholarships and study abroad opportunities for Omani students to study at leading international institutions. This not only enhances their educational experience but also enables them to serve as cultural ambassadors, promoting understanding and dialogue between Oman and the international community.

Hosting international students and scholars: Oman also welcomes international students and scholars to its educational institutions, providing them with opportunities to immerse themselves in Omani culture and contribute to the intellectual life of the country. This exchange of ideas and perspectives fosters greater cross-cultural understanding and strengthens ties between Oman and other nations.

PROMOTING PEACE AMONG YOUNGER GENERATIONS:

Youth-oriented programs: Oman recognizes the importance of engaging younger generations in peacebuilding efforts and invests in youth-oriented programs that encourage dialogue, collaboration, and mutual respect. These initiatives aim to empower young people to become agents of peace, equipped with the skills, knowledge, and attitudes necessary to foster positive change in the Middle East.

Leadership development: Many of these youth programs focus on leadership development, providing young people with opportunities to build their capacity to lead and make a positive impact on their communities. By nurturing the leadership potential of the next generation, Oman seeks to create a cadre of future leaders who are committed to peace and understanding.

Interfaith dialogue and cultural exchange: Oman also promotes interfaith dialogue and cultural exchange among young people, recognizing the importance of fostering respect for diversity and promoting tolerance. By creating opportunities for youth from different religious and cultural backgrounds to interact and learn from one another, Oman helps to break down barriers and build bridges between communities.

THE ROLE OF EDUCATION AND CULTURAL EXCHANGE IN PEACEBUILDING

The transformative power of education: Education has the power to transform individuals and societies, providing people with the knowledge and skills necessary to engage in constructive dialogue, build empathy, and promote understanding. By investing in education and cultural exchange initiatives, Oman is helping to create the conditions necessary for lasting peace in the Middle East.

Building a culture of peace: By promoting cross-cultural understanding and empowering future generations to become peacemakers, Oman is actively contributing to the creation of a culture of peace in the region. This culture is characterized by mutual respect, tolerance, and a commitment to dialogue and cooperation as the preferred means for resolving disputes and addressing challenges.

COMPARING OMAN'S QUIET DIPLOMACY TO INTERVENTIONIST APPROACHES

In the complex and often tumultuous landscape of the Middle East, Oman has garnered attention for its neutral and non-interfering foreign policy, which stands in contrast to the interventionist strategies employed by other regional actors. This chapter seeks to assess the successes and limitations of Oman's quiet diplomacy compared to more interventionist approaches, drawing lessons from the Sultanate's experience that may provide valuable guidance for policymakers and stakeholders seeking to foster peace in the Middle East and beyond.

ASSESSING SUCCESSES AND LIMITATIONS:

Oman's quiet diplomacy: Oman's foreign policy, characterized by neutrality, non-interference, and mediation, has enabled the Sultanate to maintain friendly relations with a diverse array of regional actors and play a constructive role in promoting peace and stability. Oman's quiet diplomacy has helped facilitate dialogue between conflicting parties and contributed to conflict resolution in several instances, such as the Iran nuclear deal and attempts to mediate between Iran and Saudi Arabia.

Interventionist approaches: In contrast, interventionist strategies employed by other regional actors have often been driven by geopolitical competition and power dynamics, leading to the exacerbation of conflicts and instability in the region. These approaches, which may involve military intervention, proxy warfare, or economic sanctions, can have negative consequences for both the targeted countries and the broader region.

Comparative analysis: Comparing the outcomes of Oman's quiet diplomacy to interventionist approaches highlights the potential benefits and drawbacks of each strategy. While Oman's diplomatic efforts have helped promote dialogue and foster trust among regional actors, they have also faced challenges and limitations, such as slow progress and setbacks in negotiations. Interventionist strategies, on the other hand, may achieve short-term gains for certain actors but often lead to long-term negative consequences, such as increased instability and human suffering.

DRAWING LESSONS FROM OMAN'S EXPERIENCE:

The importance of neutrality and non-interference: Oman's commitment to neutrality and non-interference has allowed it to act as an impartial mediator, building trust and credibility among regional actors. This approach demonstrates the potential benefits of adopting a neutral stance in conflict resolution efforts, as it helps to facilitate constructive dialogue and reduce tensions.

The power of quiet diplomacy: Oman's quiet diplomacy highlights the value of discreet, behind-the-scenes negotiations in promoting peace and stability. This approach enables parties to engage in dialogue without the pressure of public scrutiny, which can create an environment more conducive to compromise and mutual understanding.

The role of cultural diplomacy and interfaith dialogue: Oman's emphasis on cultural diplomacy and interfaith dialogue underscores the importance of fostering respect, tolerance, and understanding among diverse religious and ethnic groups. This approach can help to break down barriers and build bridges between communities, contributing to a more harmonious regional environment.

Balancing domestic and international priorities: Oman's experience also highlights the need to balance domestic priorities, such as economic diversification, social development, and political reforms, with the pursuit of diplomatic objectives. Ensuring domestic stability and progress can enhance a nation's capacity to engage effectively in international diplomacy and contribute to peacebuilding efforts.

THE FUTURE
OF OMAN'S
PEACEMAKING ROLE

As the geopolitical landscape of the Middle East continues to evolve, Oman's role as a regional peacemaker faces new challenges and opportunities. The increasing influence of China and Russia, coupled with changing priorities of the United States, presents both potential hurdles and avenues for Oman's diplomatic efforts. This chapter aims to assess the implications of these evolving geopolitical dynamics on Oman's continued role as a regional peacemaker and examine how shifting geopolitical interests and alignments may impact the Sultanate's ability to maintain its neutral stance and effectively mediate conflicts and tensions within the region.

EVOLVING GEOPOLITICAL DYNAMICS:

China's growing presence: China's economic expansion and increasing political influence in the Middle East present both challenges and opportunities for Oman. As China seeks to expand its Belt and Road Initiative and invest in regional infrastructure projects, the Sultanate may find new avenues for economic cooperation and diplomatic engagement. However, China's growing presence could also introduce new tensions and complexities into the regional geopolitical landscape.

Russia's role in the region: Russia's involvement in the Middle East, particularly in Syria, has bolstered its influence and complicated the regional power dynamics. While Oman has historically maintained friendly relations with Russia, the potential for tensions between Moscow and other regional actors could impact Oman's ability to mediate conflicts and maintain its neutrality.

Changing priorities of the United States: The United States has long been a key player in the Middle East, with its foreign policy shaping the region's geopolitical landscape. As the United States reassesses its strategic priorities and potentially reduces its military presence in the region, Oman may need to adapt to a changing regional security environment and reassess its diplomatic relationships.

CHANGING PRIORITIES OF KEY INTERNATIONAL PLAYERS:

Geopolitical realignments: As the priorities of key international players shift, the Middle East may experience new geopolitical realignments that could affect Oman's ability to maintain its neutral stance and mediate conflicts. These realignments may create new opportunities for cooperation or exacerbate existing tensions, depending on the interests and policies of the involved actors.

The impact on Oman's diplomacy: Oman's ability to navigate these shifting dynamics and maintain its neutral, non-interfering approach will be crucial for its continued role as a regional peacemaker. The Sultanate may need to reassess its diplomatic strategies and adapt to new realities, finding ways to balance its relationships with key international players while upholding its principles of neutrality and non-interference.

Opportunities for collaboration: Despite the challenges posed by evolving geopolitical dynamics, Oman's peacemaking role could benefit from potential opportunities for collaboration with new and existing partners. Engaging with emerging powers and adapting to the changing regional landscape may enable the Sultanate to play a proactive role in shaping regional developments, contributing to peace and stability in the Middle East.

The future of Oman's peacemaking role in the Middle East will be shaped by its ability to navigate a shifting geopolitical landscape, maintain its neutral stance, and adapt to new opportunities and challenges. As the region undergoes significant transformations, the Sultanate will need to reassess its diplomatic strategies, forge new partnerships, and balance its relationships with key international players. By doing so, Oman can continue to play a vital role as a regional peacemaker, helping to promote peace and stability in a complex and often tumultuous part of the world.